Satellite Strains

Other Books by Michael Blitz

These Now & Other Poems

Suction Files

Five Days in the Electric Chair

The Spacialist

Partitions

Letters for the Living: Teaching Writing in a Violent Age
(with C. Mark Hurlbert)

Composition and Resistance
(with C. Mark Hurlbert)

Satellite Strains

Michael Blitz

LEFT HAND BOOKS

The publisher gratefully acknowledges the John W. and Clara C. Higgins Foundation for its generous support in the funding of this book.

Designed by Bryan McHugh.

Distributed by SPD, Berkeley, CA.
Left Hand Books website: lefthandbooks.com

ISBN 1-880516-31-4

Manufactured in the United States of America.

Satellite Strains

Satellite Strains

Harrison said,
"they're all love poems." &
I said, "maybe, but what
do I love?"
He said, "love poems
aren't about love.
They're about
everything else."

Satellite Strains

Out there where the ache lives
someone's name has been forgotten off the end
of my tongue
whole sentences come unglued
replacement parts keep arriving
but I keep only
the pretty boxes.

Satellite Strains

Before the children, there were sounds
like coughing
in the next room,
I'd get up to listen and
wish there were children in the next room.

There are sounds, now, like coughing.
I get up to listen. The children are in their rooms
but my house is empty.
When I drink a glass of water,
the coughing stops
but the children go on.

Satellite Strains

In his sleep my son
steals my bones.
My body moves
like water to the wall
watching him breathe and dream.

The window frames the moon-faced moon,
a boy made of light
caught short at the surface, turned
out to my eyes.
My son breathes this world deep into
the ache my heart ignores—
to think the moon he sees
is late for the night watch,
late as I will be late
when he is a man.

The sun is caught behind the moon tonight,
as my son is caught within my eyes,
defracted at the edges,
his face glows with the light of a promise
his birth has forced from me—
nine years ago to tell him
now the moon's truth is half in darkness
as a son's life is lit by only half
his father's time.

Satellite Strains

…the cruelties…
all those
stories
from the cracked photograph,
in memory,
a place where
pain washed
children's children,
the dead
are nowhere.

Glass world—
is it
this or that

which is loneliness,

a place where cruelties
are stories
men and women
remember by whispering.

It's cold,
it's raining,
the storm
elsewhere,
paper
and people,
yourself, or your father,
how easy it is
to use the
cold and the dark.
Follow them
in your body.

That night
it was a pencil
until there was a head,
so simple.
In the rainy street
there was nothing
but a man, a corner,
a woman, a doorway,
a cigarette,
smoke,
dark buildings,
the weight of a specific sadness—
the head
passed.

Writing
at this very moment
is the same
you can go for a walk
impatient not to feel
so certain,
to figure out
what to say.
My friend
clawed at the cruelties,
a piece of evidence,
the way she trembled
almost like a bargain we'd made—
and then the streets
when it's over,
changed.

You cannot turn
glass
out of the
scar

that is a life.
Mostly it's nothing
you can imagine
this and that
or more glass
on the piano—
you'd think
it's time to plan
for something to happen.

This time
what stayed was
a father with a child—
what can I say?—
it becomes ordinary
to say anything.
Only the window
is mistaken
for this world.

Satellite Strains

Even "no one home"
is something there—
an empty house full of
voices or a head
throbbing with noise—
incessant clatter of film
on sprockets
young faces leap out of old light
half of a lens cap
cuts off half of a life—
Even the stillness fades
and the soundless piano
swims up into a dream of
aching for a fistful of sentences
that will turn the pounding to prayer—
someone there
in the cropped photographs
is gone—
a pair of hands
from the edge of the frame
reaches for a child whose adulthood lies
in ambush—
Even now
the odd drifting into memory
shatters like a dropped mirror
the fragments still staring up from the floor
wheel upon wheel of still images
scrolled across a hot lamp—
jagged dances of children
—which eyes watch now?—
alone in the thin light of a strange room,
looking at the end of one history
and into the inverted focus of a new one—

fathers of sons and daughters give themselves
Even odds that
the children at the door
will knock
or knock it down
just to know if the "no one home"
is over.

Satellite Strains

Into the cup
but keeping the fatness separate
ingredients for a thing I thought
to drink
but I didn't
know where the fat was
going
to go so
I put it outside and now it keeps
rubbing against the glass I use
to keep things from
crashing out of the room.

Satellite Strains

System of cut off
cut down
a vein
hooks and fingers
"come on, now
come on out, now"
every in
is out of me—how did it
get detached
a cold looking around
catch that
here-it-comes
before blacking out
"come on, now"
throat cracking
someone laughing
"come on out, now" laughing
system of attachments
cut off
slack-tongued
dry-boned
"come on now come on out, now"
catch that
look,
"stay awake, now,"
catch that
look,
"stay awake, now,
crack it out black, now
come on out, now"
out of me.

Satellite Strains

A curse in a box
forces you.
The flux of your slacks
creases you.
The rack of cut meat
reduces you.
A list on the door
accosts you.

Satellite Strains

Either
it is
me or I
am it—all possible
information so-
designated—
it or
NOT it—
the two hands
containing only one or
two bits, either
the left or
what is
left—
so it was
with you: either you
were or were not
fully informed, containing
one or two hands, or
yourself, not to speak of it—
the phonograph spins
obsolete information,
turning on a strict nostalgia, as if
forgotten
as you have been either
forgotten or have
gotten yourself stuck in
formation
the way your hands hung about you,
I cannot recall
how long I am supposed to
keep you in mind this way—some days
I am at once aware that I have remembered

your first words which were
NOT the first words you said,
but the words
which I heard first, one time
you said it
quickly and in a strict sense I heard
something else—
                    —later
it became what I now
remember you having said, despite
the unbearable silence of knowing that
I have begun to forget you.

Satellite Strains

We are approaching
ceaseless alphabets
unequal to the task—
having to live out
this sentence,
having begun it, it
goes away beneath the hand.

The language you
use (of use)
suggests you; it is
not you, nor
used to you—it
has only you to thank.

Use revokes the sentence.
The sentence is
"in use" but it
contains nothing:
nothing (of use)
is "in the sentence."
One says "the
sentence" referring
to the contrary.

For example, someone has already
killed you and now
thinks it can't
happen just that way;
and so each time
the plot changes; the result
is the same and
each time, the same
thought that the

actual events can't possibly work out
that way. Every day,
after someone kills you, someone
must try again. In this
sentence, you never die.

Satellite Strains

It was only an effect of
rising so
quickly everyone knew that nothing
like a man bound so
loosely
had ever fallen to
the street that way but he was
still falling down where the street was.

Satellite Strains

Was it breakfast you had been forgetting
coming down the stairs, looking puzzled,
or that you had been upstairs at all,
finding out
what I was keeping there?
It might have been yours one day had you stopped
your incessant measurement of
the contours of
my head.

Instead, your tongue is dry and split,
you raise your glass and smile your teeth
into the staccato of syllables you force
into a sentence—
no one is listening closely enough to catch
the catch in your voice when you see
no one can remember
who you are.

Satellite Strains

Yes, the crack in the earth denotes an
odd tease,
a hatch to the heart,
a sore neck, or a sick need,
the joke is no one sees
the ditch as the
ditch—
they try one door and then
another and think it's
art
and I, too, notice the day is as
dry as a
dry scar,
a hot sheet, or a
rash across the head—
the chair crashes as a jar does, and
I can say "sorry" yet others say
I rant in the strained tones I don't
deny.

Satellite Strains

whispered magic...
murmuring
the kiss of
all promises
taste of dates
as old as
grace
grows
vines
as thick
as fish.

Satellite Strains

There, there were words and a tongue beneath them—
"there, there"—and a tongue around me—
there and there—
no need to say so—
stitch your fingers to my tongue
so I don't swallow your gestures—
language is a belly full of Siamese twins.

Satellite Strains

It rains you see
a window and the glass
of something brown on the counter
a spoon
a pack of matches
gets confusing for a moment
it's not clear what it is
you were about to do.

It rains and you see a window
the door opens and it is
your foot
across the saddle but
whose hand closing
on the counter
a broken glass
matches the
broken window your hand
is making.

It rains like a window
breaking around you
your head on the counter
brown grout between the tiles
a foot at the door
kicks you open.

It rains when the window opens
you left the matches outside but
they burn
pieces of glass on the counter
are wet from crying
one match for each piece
burning.

It rains but you aren't home
broken into pieces
left outside
wet and burning
like a broken window
around your head.

Satellite Strains

A face as easy as a leaf flies—
seems so close…
calls my lies "a file"—says
"come fill me."

I lose my sail,
some silly coil of lace
says "fill me"—
I fall off.

My smile is facile—
my eyes smell of oil.
Life is as small as mice.

Some say allies may come as
flies scale a flame—
as loyal as a seal.

My face comes off—
I call my life a meal of lies—
"come film me."

Satellite Strains

Hands you withdraw
from the catastrophe are
still twitching, still raw,
still yours.

Satellite Strains

(A leap—
        pull—
a hall, chill,
a cheap wall
                home/
                        hell/
how we ache—
mice, a lame mule, owl,
a wheel, map…
                        a heap.

We will chop a hole.
We will lie.
We will howl.

We mail a lost
tale—some
claim to last choices—
the tastes we sell.
Who chooses late,
chooses to
cast out the
shot souls—
those who paste
solace to thistle,
        stitch bottles to a sheet,
                sleep as wet cattle—
stop to attach
a heel to toe,
to hoist the sail—
we seethe at the mast, but
it's a piece of lace.

All a daze,

we allow whole patches to
set the teeth,
to be the loom we use,
to be at the satellite as it
seals us out.)

Satellite Strains

Let it wait—
a late "waltz"—
label it ice,
call it a law,
table it—
claw at a lace wall,
a wet web,
bite it,
eat it,
it will be
a lie we tell.

Satellite Strains

An ark was an awkward idea—
rains end,
one's own dead rise
or die anew as a rose
is adored—
I know a swan was done
as a work
on a desk—
a sad ode
on a wise oak—
I swore in an ear no one
saw—
'we are done in—
—no oars.'

Satellite Strains

You know that

fine set of fine lies so thin one knows one's words only as a
device for tripping into an accident of candor,

& that

each time entails one
chance, though
everyone
wants two—

& that

the dancer is also
the dance & the singer
is the song,
the beaten are also
the killers,
& you raise your hands
as if to make something
happen
& all that happens
is someone runs away
the doers
are the done,
maybe there really is one chance
each time
a different step
into the same puddle of
words
the poets are the poems
they write
when nothing else
sounds like a verb,

actors & the actions
blurring into a glass of bourbon,
the drinkers are drunk
& the dreamers disappear
in the end of a nightmare,
a man sits up in bed
grateful to be awake,
fearful that another
is dreaming his gratitude,
nearing the end of yet another dream
or the dance
into the night that lasts forever
for every second
you can hold on to the words
to describe it,
it is you, singing
& you in the song,
your life is the lie the liar tells,
& you are the killer
of time,
it is always you as the word designs
a world of others to keep you company,
a gathering of hands that gather
you around a center of something
that looks familiar,
feels like the dark, soft edges around
a memory that you are certain you are
just
now
making
history has always been
a set-up

& you know that all lies
rely
on an equal mix of truth & desire,

it is painful to be hungry for the details of a life
you have invented—

—not that
   lying isn't also praying.

Satellite Strains

yes, I lie—
my smile is
sly, my eye is
ice—
sell me

Satellite Strains

Roses go to salt as
mercy is ageless—
as dates are
tales made old &
days go
as easy as a
lost rattle.

Some rage at
a gray storm,
he starts to—
she hates to—
he rides it to
a rodeo,
to taste a last
glory,
she goes late to
see his mastery go
stale—
he tries to say,
"come to me"—
she retorts,
"my time has
come"—
he sees she is
already cold.

A rose lets a
tree die
as a rag stays
tied to a leg.
Some trees &
some legs are
greedy, yet

some are ready
to retire.
Mercy is a test
as grace &
remorse are.

A girl reads her
diary to her older
sister.
She cries &
her tears are darts,
her sister
comes to her
as a rose to its
artist—
she says,
"Some roses
are eagles."

He is tired as he sees
eagles rise.
A girl is told
stories tied to
dry grass & her days
are roses
tied to a great
eagle as it soars.

Satellite Strains

All despair has, as its other side,
its dissolution and the dissolve
itself is the other side of the dark
surface of a skin you cannot wear.

You cannot bear to let go of an empty
hand when it is clear it is not your own,
but there never was a hand where the
emptiness is
only the other side of the back of your
tongue where the last word
you didn't say
comes back to cancel the others.

You are left with a silence that takes up
too many syllables at the tips of your
fingers, your subtlest gestures measure
an echo you have only just begun to
hear as your own first words at the edge
of the argument
that is your mouth
endlessly ruptured.

Satellite Strains

You feel light
and strange
as she asks
why leave
    this time
your father
will throw his
shadow like a
secret across
a dreamless winter
he whispers
I am not through
roaring at the child
you were
    for her
it is over
and the dark
snow falls
like a story
into sleep

Satellite Strains

One man she anchors
in a camera—
some cameras lie.

Each man she moors
near her,
each one calls her
home.

Her air reaches shore
as an ache,
more rain
means she lies
near.

Someone is also
her shame.
She has chosen him
as her charm.

His lies are noise in her ears.
She can erase him.
Her camera is a lance.

She is on
ice.
Someone calls me.
I hear "Michael"—
I hear noise—
Each ear recoils.

Soon, her aches are
in me, also.
No, I lie.
I can erase her—

no camera,
no rich, cool oils can
reach her.

Satellite Strains

One is oneself one's
own
fledgling
hand puppet

as an organization of one's life
young girls did
the twist at the
altar.

Satellite Strains

On the High Holy Days,
I edged into a dark place among
dark robes, uncut sidelocks,
unbathed, small-thumbed, child-handed
men in one of a hundred
Crown Heights synagogues
and stood to murmur Kaddish
for one who'd once said
she would become Jewish
if it would make my life easier—
but it was her *life*
I wanted—
yisgadal, v'yiskadash shemai raba…

I do not belong here,
but this prayer, this time,
belongs to this place
in my mouth,
the rabbi saw me murmuring
and nodded as if only my grief
mattered,
yisgadal, v'yiskadash shemai raba…

When I stood by her hospital bed, her head
in white bandages, her body covered,
sewn through by miles of tubes and wires,
I knew the body in that bed
wasn't her,
and that I didn't belong there.
And when I got the phone call that she was gone,
I pictured her turning her own switches off,
watching her monitor go flat,
tucking the bedsheets around herself
with broken hands,

stepping back, solemnly and murmuring
Kaddish
    yisgadal, v'yiskadash shemai raba,
to make my life easier.

& the old man beside me, pointing
to the words in the book—
"we are here," he said,
"we are here."

Satellite Strains

even the quality of the sadness is a matter
of taste
or the matter, when you ask
what is.

Satellite Strains

...from kevod hechai[1] to
kevod ha-met[2]...
....halvayat ha-met[3]

the schomer's[4] eyes are ruined,
the suicide's place is lost,
both wear the tachrichim[5]...

both tear the Kaddish[6] from our throats.

[1] The care of the living
[2] The treatment of the dead
[3] The escorting of the dead
[4] The one who watches the dead and recites the psalms
[5] The cloth of the dead
[6] The prayer of the dead

Satellite Strains

knowledge of your sorrows
doesn't equal sorrow
still
you know what you know and
remember the rise and wash of grief
as if grief itself was your soul
what the letters spell
is not the same
as the letter's spell
as if the rise and fall of each pen stroke
falters in your reading of the choked
remarks
later you know again the choking
was your own
and the words on the page
lie shattered
into syllables you cannot reassemble
or
later you know again the choking on the page
was your own shattered assembly
of a soul you cannot recover
your soul and the soul you
remember
out of the nagging sadness that
spells a life

had there been a message
to which your reply
might complete a circuit
spun out of rage
the silence of which might rise
in the rise of your capital letters
your names for the sorrows

whose names do not equal the grief they require
had there been a time you didn't cry out of your dream
the same broken matters your life resembles
had you once distinguished between light and
longing
you could forget your desire to turn letters
to whispers
and words sick with wanting you have
had to cut loose from who you are

Satellite Strains

To go there
one goes
off
as a great rabbit,
bent on bearing a
great thing or a
smart gift in
one fist,
to get the first good
taste of
something bright and
mean.

Satellite Strains

Across the grid her excellent sounds

divide the space into arms and strings

she drives an anchor bolt into the neck ring just to.

Satellite Strains

"We made a pact"—
an act of disabling proportions
not to love one another—
the truer I stay the more
my life aches—
do we make such promises
just to wear ourselves out
into sleep—
in these empty hands
I see the promise has cut
lifelines
into ladders.

Satellite Strains

Here are things whose things have taught me.
A single wire
stitched through the torso
catches functions circles make.
A tube in back through which to catch you
now you have these things for breaking.
Nothing fixes places to you.
These are thinking things.
Refuse them.

There were things remembered for you,
photographs and wooden boxes
over your objections to them,
shown to you in early evening.
These are things you once desired,
a torso full of spent emotion,
an arrow with your skin around it,
love without vocabulary,
dreamless sleep to break the needing.
These are restless things.
Align them.

Under oath you call things names
for which your memory aches, recalling
choices, now, you'd once forgotten—
time to change them long since over,
speaking now seems too much like
another layer of imprecision, still
to be precise requires your stillness.
Single words have lasted lifetimes,
tangled speeches wrap around an old desire
for causing trouble—
these are troubling things,
or are they

things at all—
refuse to live them.

And at the corner of attention,
things are moving past your knowing.
Lethal interruptions daily make
a single sound's erasure final—
vague piano nagging near you,
sounds you've never heard
now cancel something useful.
These are things
you can't recall
by speaking of them.

Here are things, then, long distorted,
wired into mind like facts, your pulse
can't measure, lies like doorways,
every word the work of fracture.
There are things long held in tension
cracking now along the sight line.
These are things that whisper *"tell me"*—
say the word that things
require.

Satellite Strains

Then I could construct the end of it.
Instead, every desire
is a description of the world.
You said a day without another long proposition
between us felt like a kiss
in a foreign language.
I thought the truth was an extreme case of
navigation, breathless and proper.
The surface licks back at us
as though we are an application of dry ink
to activate,
everything would be all right
if we hadn't been running across
the whiteness,
the rain made for quarrelling,
and everything else became a fiction.

Satellite Strains

A lazy day
and a lady—
a daze

no deal on a lemon
one model day—
no demon

"alone" and
"lonely"
all done

one day and
a dozen
all mean no
need,
only a
nod—

one lady,
one May day,
one lone name all
amaze me.

Satellite Strains

No arms but those.

Not now anymore.
Never now.
I've never been there
where now
was.

Now, never,
I'm always here
where I last was,
straining
to be elsewhere.

Satellite Strains

Projection consoles the image
—the whip of
recognition—as if the mirror hands
you your fear of being
looked at.

The length of this day becomes a
decoration
the tattoo artist forgets himself clear
through
to the esophagus
to teach me
that place for these things.

Satellite Strains

As if one
could
make light
for two.

As if (this)
one would make light
of two.

How does one make room
for (this) making
we do?

Satellite Strains

This morning sure
it was that dream-sheer
bluffing that
I could stand you
saying it all over again, but this time no
cement mattress covering the door
falling around me in the springs and wires
someone said I made it up
everything I made
I made it
I made everything up I can't believe you
can't you believe I could make it
up
make it up
can't you make it up
for me

Satellite Strains

The stomach ache after
the loss of that
safe tale—

is this roar I hear
me?

It amazes...
that breath attaches itself to echoes,
or that the force of assault is less
if I miss her.

The braille of her
tall reach
touches this scar—

She stitches her
home to me—
it hatches
a chorus.

She hates a mess
if it is also a
cure.

Later,
a letter,
a list of catches,
a chart of our failure to
scare the oaths
out of our mouths.

Satellite Strains

For one singularity
I would give two of everything else.

Satellite Strains

I have cut myself
no slack.
I have to cut myself to see if I'll bleed
words I need
to live by.
I have had to cut myself
in line so I'll get
to the front faster.
I'll have to cut myself short
just to finish on time.
I'm cutting my time down to
lines, false fronts, words and blood
to make a golem of it.

Satellite Strains

They want to get down to size
to get IN there again
maybe to move all this death around to find out
what my life was doing
with all those things you thought you had
lost.

Satellite Strains

It comes down to
bringing it all
up.

Satellite Strains

Each time, each moment, the first second
and then the second,
one chance for
one time,
one chance
for all time,
"one chance each time"—
each times each equals
this time now

something—
          —what is it?—
I've been asking
forever, now,
for you.

Satellite Strains

First, it rusts.
I lift it—
as if I must—
& it's lost.

I sit as if it
hurts,
as if trust
is a rash.
I sift that ash
& it stirs—
it's a rat that's
at fault.

At last, this
is a start.

SATELLITE STRAINS

NO
MORE
MORE
OF
THAT
ONLY
LESS
THIS
IS
NOT
TO
SAY
MORE
IS—
OR
LESS
IS
BEST
ONLY

THAT
NO
LOSS
GOES
WITHOUT
SAYING
THAT
SAID
THE
LESS
LEFT
THE
BETTER
THIS
WAY
WANT
HAS
NO
MORE
THAN
ITSELF

TO
WANT
TO
GO
ON
OF
ITS
OWN
ACCORD
THIS
TERRIBLE
AIMLESSNESS
THAT
HAS
NO
HISTORY
ONLY
NOW
THE
DISABLING
LESSENING

RINGING
THAT
LOOSENS
SYLLABLES
INTO
TEETH
DROPPING
INTO
THAT
OPEN
WHITENESS
WHAT
THIS
LONELINESS
WANTS
THAT
COMES
ACROSS
THE
WIRES
PASSED

THROUGH
THE
EYE
OF
THE
PUPPET
THE
HAND
BECOMES
GESTURES
TOWARD
THE
SINGULAR
ACHE
NO
MORE
LISTENING
FOR
BROKEN
FINGERS
NO

LESSENING
OF
DESIRE
FOR
AN
END
TO
DESIRE
OR
TO
WANT
ONLY
A
SINGLE
BIT
OF
TWINE
ALONG
SIDE
THE
ONE

NERVE
FIRING
THE
ONE
STING
OF
MEMORY
WHOSE
WIRES
CAN
NOT
BE
CLIPPED
AND
THE
STRING
TO
TIE
IT
UP
THE

BUNDLE
TO
BE
LEFT
OUTSIDE
NEAR
THE
WROUGHT-
IRON
RAILS
FROM
WHICH
CLOTHING
AND
SHOES
AND
THE
OCCASIONAL
GLIMPSE
OF
PERSONAL

TASTES
HANG
UNTIL
MID-
DAWN
WHEN
THOSE
WHOSE
WANT
IS
FAR
GREATER
COME
FOR
A
TASTE
OF
A
GLANCE
FROM
THE

HIGH
WINDOWS
THE
EYES
LIKE
LOCKED
SOCKETS
TOGETHER
A
SINGLE
STRAND
OF
LONELINESS
CONNECTS
THEM
BUT
THE
LIFT
OF
LIGHT
DARKENS

THE
FACES
OF
NEED
ONE
HURRIES
OFF
THE
OTHER
HURRIES
FURTHER
INSIDE
NOT
ONE
WORD
NOR
ONE
THOUSAND
WOULD
CHANGE
THIS

LACK
TO
HAVING
ENOUGH
HAVING
KEPT
ITSELF
LACKING
ALL
BUT
ITS
OWN
VOCABULARY
NOW
THE
HAVING
FINDS
ITSELF
WITHOUT
HAVING
TO

AND
WANTS
ONLY
NOW
TO
LOSE
ITSELF
TO
KEEPING
THE
WORDS
AWAY
FROM
THE
EMPTY
CENTER
WHOSE
NAMELESSNESS
HAS
BEEN
THE

ONE
CLEAR
HOUR
OF
SLEEP
EACH
NIGHT
OF
WHAT
POSSIBLE
USE
IS
INCESSANT
MEMORY
BUT
TO
STRAIN
EVEN
THE
TIGHTEST
ROPE

AROUND
THE
CUT
NECK
OF
SADNESS
OUT
THERE
WHERE
THE
TROUBLES
BOIL
AS
IF
DISCONNECTED
FROM
THE
HAND
THAT
STIRS
THEM

NOTHING
CAN
BE
PULLED
THIS
TAUT
AND
STILL
BE
ITSELF
A
DARK
THREAD
TURNS
WHITE
THEN
DISAPPEARS
STEEL
CABLE
UNRAVELS
AND

SPRINGS
BACK
ALONG
ITS
LENGTH
AN
ARM
PULLS
FREE
OF
ITS
SOCKET
AND
IS
NEITHER
ARM
NOR
BODY
BUT
A
MODEL

FOR
AN
AUTOMATIC
WEAPON
NOT
EVEN
A
CHAIN
OF
DNA
MAINTAINS
COHESION
UNDER
STRAIN
BECOMES
INSTEAD
A
GENETIC
CONUNDRUM
BUT
THIS

CHAIN
OF
EVENTS
THAT
HAS
BEEN
THE
GLUE
BETWEEN
DAYS
GOES
ON
THE
DISTANCE
DRAWING
A
SHUDDER
FROM
ITS
MOST
DISTANT

MUSCLE
IS
THERE
SOME
RAZOR
THAT
CUTS
ACROSS
THESE
EMPTY
LINES
OR
MAKES
A
SCAR
FROM
A
CATASTROPHE
AND
IF
IT

DID
WOULD
IT
CHANGE
THE
RADIATING
PHANTOM
PAINS
INTO
FIREFLIES
IN
A
THICK
BOTTLE
TO
STOP
THE
FLICKER
OF
SKIN-
CRAWLING

FINGERS
ALONG
THE
BACK
OF
THE
ROOM
WHERE
THE
SOUND
OF
YOUR
OWN
VOICE
DRAPES
ITSELF
LIKE
A
DAMP
SHROUD
AROUND

ONLY
THE
CONTOURS
OF
YOUR
BODY
YOUR
BODY
ITSELF
SOMEPLACE
YOU
CAN'T
FIND
IT
BECAUSE
YOU
WERE
MISTAKEN
WHEN
YOU
THOUGHT

YOU
WOULD
REMEMBER
WHERE
YOU
PUT
IT.

Michael Blitz was born in New York City in 1958. *Satellite Strains* is his sixth book of poetry. He has also co-authored two books with C. Mark Hurlbert: *Letters for the Living: Teaching Writing in a Violent Age* (NCTE Press, 1998) and *Composition and Resistance* (Boynton/Cook Heinemann, 1991). His poems have appeared in literary and scholarly journals, and his essays have been published in journals and books on cultural studies, rhetoric and composition, popular culture, and poetics. He is currently Professor of English and Chair of Thematic Studies at John Jay College of Criminal Justice of The City University of New York. He lives in New York with his wife, Mozelle Dayan, and their children, Daina and Cory Blitz and Celine and Rene Dayan-Bonilla.